A GIFT FOR AN

Ḥaḍrat Mirza Ghulam Ahmad
of Qadian[as]

The Promised Messiah and Mahdi
Founder of the Aḥmadiyyah Muslim Jamā'at

ISLAM INTERNATIONAL PUBLICATIONS LIMITED

A Gift for An-Nadwah
English translation of
Tuḥfatun-Nadwah (Urdu)
by Ḥaḍrat Mirza Ghulam Ahmad of Qadian,
the Promised Messiah and Mahdi[as].

First Edition (Urdu): Qadian 1902
English Edition: UK 2010

Published by:
Islam International Publications Ltd.
'Islamabad' Sheephatch Lane,
Tilford, Surrey GU10 2AQ
United Kingdom

Printed in UK at:
Raqeem Press
'Islamabad'
Tilford, Surrey GU10 2AQ

ISBN: 978-1-84880-053-3

CONTENTS

Introduction v

Publishers' Note ix

At-Tablīgh 1

A Poem by Mīr Nāṣir Nawāb Ṣāḥib of Dehli 5

A Gift for An-Nadwah 9

A Reason to Rejoice for All Muslims and Those who Seek the Truth 29

Index 33

بِسۡمِ اللّٰہِ الرَّحۡمٰنِ الرَّحِیۡمِ

INTRODUCTION

ABOUT THE AUTHOR

Born in 1835 in Qadian (India), Ḥaḍrat Mirza Ghulam Ahmad, the Promised Messiah and Mahdi[as], devoted himself to the study of the Holy Quran and to a life of prayer and contemplation. Finding Islam the constant target of theological attacks and the fortunes of the Muslims at a low ebb, he undertook the vindication and exposition of Islam. In his vast corpus of writings (including his *Magnus Opus Barāhīn-e-Aḥmadiyyah*), his lectures, discourses, religious debates etc., he argued that Islam was a living faith and the only religion capable of establishing a relationship between man and his creator. The teachings contained in the Holy Quran and the Law promulgated by Islam were designed to raise man to moral, intellectual and spiritual perfection. He announced that God had appointed him the Messiah and Mahdi as mentioned in the prophecies of the Bible, the Holy Quran and Hadith. In 1889 he began to accept initiates into the Aḥmadiyyah Jamā'at. The Jama'at which he founded is now established in almost two hundred countries. His eighty books are written mostly in Urdu, but a significant proportion of his writings are also in Arabic and Persian.

ABOUT THE BOOK

By 1902, over two decades had elapsed since the Promised

Messiah[as] started publishing and widely circulating the revelations he received from God. He presented them as proof of his claim, arguing that if he had been an impostor, falsely attributing hundreds of revelations to God, the Almighty would not have given him such a lengthy reprieve in keeping with the warning mentioned in the Holy Quran. Instead, God Almighty had blessed him with countless signs of His support and brought disgrace upon his opponents.

It was against this backdrop that Ḥāfiẓ Muḥammad Yūsuf published a public announcement contending that there was nothing unique in this claim, for there had been many liars and impostors in the past who had lived many years after making their false claims and died a natural death.

In response to this announcement, the Promised Messiah[as] addressed the ulema of An-Nadwah through a short but incisive treatise entitled *A Gift for An-Nadwah* which was published on 6th October 1902. He forcefully rejected Muḥammad Yūsuf's contention and argued that it contravened the clear purport of the Holy Quran. Not only that, but if Muḥammad Yūsuf's thesis were to be accepted there would be no means by which to distinguish false claimants from true ones.

The book opens with an Arabic preface entitled At-Tablīgh in which the Promised Messiah[as] invites the ulema of An-Nadwah to the judgment of the Holy Quran and presents before them his claim of being the Promised Messiah and Mahdi[as]. In order to distinguish the preface from the main body of the text and to express the difference of style and language, the Arabic prose has been conveyed in a more archaic style of English and set in italic type.

The book closes with a short epilogue on the discovery of a new piece of evidence regarding the death of Jesus Christ.

ACKNOWLEDGMENTS

I would like to express my appreciation for the help and support given by Maulana Munir-ud-din Shams Sahib, Additional Wakīlut-Taṣnīf, London and Dr. Muhammad Shafiq Sehgal Sahib, for their valuable suggestions and their help in bringing out this book.

I owe a debt of gratitude to the following who worked diligently in the various stages of this translation: Mirza Usman Ahmad Adam, Raja Ata-ul-Mannan, Qaḍi M.J. As'ad, Syed Tanwir Mujtaba and Tahir Mahmood Mubashar.

Chaudhary Muhammad Ali
Wakīlut-Taṣnīf
Rabwah
5 June 2010

PUBLISHERS' NOTE

The words in the text in normal brackets () and in between the long dashes—are the words of the Promised Messiah[as] and if any explanatory words or phrases are added by the translator for the purpose of clarification, they are put in square brackets [ ].

The name of Muhammad[sa], the Holy Prophet of Islam, has been followed by the symbol [sa], which is an abbreviation for the salutation *Ṣallallāhu 'Alaihi Wasallam* (may peace and blessings of Allah be upon him). The names of other Prophets and Messengers are followed by the symbol [as], an abbreviation for *'Alaihissalām* (on whom be peace). The actual salutations have not generally been set out in full, but they should nevertheless, be understood as being repeated in full in each case. The symbol [ra] is used with the name of the companions of the Holy Prophet[sa] and those of the Promised Messiah[as]. It stands for *Raḍi Allāhu 'anhu/'anhā/'anhum* (May Allah be pleased with him/with her/with them). [rh] stands for *Raḥimahullāhu Ta'ālā* (may Allah have mercy on him). [at] stands for *Ayyadahullāhu Ta'ālā* (May Allah, the Mighty help him).

In transliterating Arabic words we have followed the following system adopted by the Royal Asiatic Society.

ا	at the beginning of a word, pronounced as *a, i, u* preceded by a very slight aspiration, like *h* in the English word 'honour'.
ث	*th,* pronounced like th in the English word 'thing'.
ح	*ḥ,* a guttural aspirate, stronger than h.
خ	*kh,* pronounced like the Scotch ch in 'loch'.

ذ *dh*, pronounced like the English th in 'that'.

ص *ṣ*, strongly articulated s.

ض *ḍ*, similar to the English th in 'this'.

ط *ṭ*, strongly articulated palatal t.

ظ *ẓ*, strongly articulated z.

ع ', a strong guttural, the pronunciation of which must be learnt by the ear.

غ *gh*, a sound approached very nearly in the r '*grasseye*' in French, and in the German r. It requires the muscles of the throat to be in the 'gargling' position whilst pronouncing it.

ق *q*, a deep guttural k sound.

ئ ', a sort of catch in the voice.

Short vowels are represented by:

a for ـــَـــ (like *u* in 'bud');

i for ـــِـــ (like *i* in 'bid');

u for ـــُـــ (like *oo* in 'wood');

Long vowels by:

ā for ـــَاـــ or آ (like *a* in 'father');

ī for ی ـــِـــ or ـــِیـــ (like *ee* in 'deep');

ū for و ـــُـــ (like *oo* in 'root');

Other:

ai for ی ـــَـــ (like *i* in 'site')♦;

au for و ـــَـــ (resembling *ou* in 'sound').

In transliterated words the letter 'e' is to be pronounced as

---

♦In Arabic words like شيخ(Shaikh) there is an element of diphthong which is missing when the word is pronounced in Urdu.

in 'prey' which rhymes with 'day'; however the pronunciation is flat without the element of English diphthong. If in Urdu and Persian words 'e' is lengthened a bit more it is transliterated as 'ei' to be pronounced as 'ei' in 'feign' without the element of diphthong thus 'کے' is transliterated as 'Kei'. For the nasal sound of 'n' we have used the symbol 'ń'. Thus Urdu word 'میں' is transliterated as 'meiń'.*

The consonants not included in the above list have the same phonetic value as in the principal languages of Europe.

We have not transliterated Arabic words which have become part of the English language, e.g., Islam, Mahdi, Quran**, Hijra, Ramadan, Hadith, ulema, umma, sunna, kafir, pukka etc.

For quotes straight commas (straight quotes) are used to differentiate them from the curved commas used in the system of transliteration, ' for ع, ' for ء. Commas as punctuation marks are used according to the normal usage. Similarly for apostrophe normal usage is followed.

Publishers

* These transliterations are not included in the system of transliteration by Royal Asiatic Society. [Publishers]

** Concise Oxford Dictionary records Quran in three forms—Quran, Qur'an and Koran. [Publishers]

AT-TABLĪGH

O' people of Nadwah! Come to that which is common between us. Let us agree that the Holy Quran is our arbiter and accept only that which conforms to the words of the Gracious God.

O' ye who are unmindful! Certainly, Islam is the true religion and all guidance has been perfected in the Holy Quran. Its teaching alone is everlasting and worthy of preservation. It holds the secrets of the future and the accounts of the past. Wouldst thou accept anything other than the Holy Quran?

Behold, all good is in the Quran, and most evil is that which contradicts it. O' righteous ones, all that is contrary to its narrative and guidance should be cast aside, for such things are welcome only to the transgressors.

I am the Messiah. I walk with the truth and beckon towards God. I beseech thee for the sake of my Lord and warn thee of His wrath. Will thou not take heed? I am come to thee from my Lord with manifest signs and have been taught that which thou hast not, and have seen that which thou seest not. Wouldst thou treat me as a liar without coming to me with thy queries?

Christ has surely died. Thou will not succeed in bringing him to life. O' foolish souls, falsify not the Holy

Quran. If Jesus is to come before the Day of Judgement as thou would believe, why will he deny all knowledge of the fall of the Christians? As thou hast read, Christ will confess his ignorance and say that he knew not of the innovations they adopted after him. Had he returned to the world and seen what they did, Christ should have spoken thus; O' my Lord, I was returned to the world by Thy command and lived among my people for forty years. I found them venerating my mother and I. They were adamant in their resolve. Thus, I broke the cross and corrected [the errors of] their age. Many of them I slew and they humbled themselves and submitted to the faith of the Lord.

Ask thy Jesus why he will utter falsehoods on the Day of Judgement. He will hide his testimony and be from among the ignorant.

By God, I am come from Him. If you are righteous then honour the oath taken in Allah's name. I have been given many signs and the Holy Quran has closed all paths except mine. Where will be thy flight?

As thou dost know I come at the head of the century. The moon and the sun were eclipsed in the month of Ramadan so that they may serve as two signs from my Gracious Lord in my favour. He raised the plague so that people would think and ponder. What has overcome thee that thou do not see the signs of Allah. Or maybe thou art displeased with what thy eyes behold.

O people! I have with me testimonies from God. Will thou not believe? I possess signs from my Lord. Will thou not submit? O' ye that make haste, if thou were to begin to count these testimonies thou wouldst fail in thy endeavour. Therefore, become righteous.

Whenever any messenger cometh unto thee with a teaching that pleases thee not, thou treat some of them as liars and shed the blood of others. I am supported by my Lord, but O' deceitful ones, thou art not. Have thy edicts of death and false accusations before the courts caused me to perish? Art thou not ashamed. God has decreed that He and His Messengers will triumph. Hearken ye wagers of battle, thou cannot humble God.

I swear by God that I am truthful. I am not like those who invent lies. Dost thou seek to reject me, despite the absolute proof I have shown to thee? Will thou not return to thy Lord? Or will thou find everlasting life with thy Messiah?

Dost thou not read the Chapters Nūr, Taḥrīm *and* Fātiḥah*? Or dost their recitation displease thee and thou think that it concerns thee not?*

O people of Nadwah. To thee I write this letter, that it may open thy eyes before the respite of the Lord is lifted and thou canst offer a defence or struggle with me further. I have named it 'A Gift for An-Nadwah'*. I give it unto thee and await to see thy response.*

I pray , O Allah, make this book a source of blessing for those who behave without arrogance.

O Allah, be Thou a witness that I have delivered the message with which I was charged and count me among those who deliver Thy message without fear.

Āmīn, O' Lord Āmīn.

A Poem by Mīr Nāṣir Nawāb Ṣāḥib of Dehli

Noah's Ark, an invitation to faith
A book of outstanding grace and beauty.

A single reading can revive belief
And illumine the light of conviction.

A thing purer than the water of life
The dead are brought to life by its nectar.

Bereft of the words to speak its glory,
How am I to articulate its praise?

A beacon for the lost and the adrift
A means for their direction, their guidance.

Supporting the helpless, the feeble weak
Providing refuge for the desperate.

With content matchless in magnificence
A sign of the Messenger of the Lord.

Unravelling the mysteries of faith
To those who follow its words carefully.

Ignorance gives way to knowledge and truth
Hastening the flight of superstition.

This is a garden of heaven, not earth
In which walk maidens and eternal youth.

Where rivers of milk and honey flow forth
Past citadels of breathtaking beauty.

Passage on this ship is free of all cost
There is no yearning for payment or charge.

We are ready to sacrifice our all
For Him Who has given us this Vessel.

O Lord, Who are Gracious and Merciful
Grant us the opportunity to serve.

Let us forsake the desires of our souls
Let Satan recoil from our company.

Let us always be dutiful to You
Let our hearts accept as true Your teaching.

Be You pleased with us, and we with You
As our souls depart this temporal frame.

Humble is Nāṣir, Your loyal servant
Who wants of You only Your protection.

Lord! Have mercy on me as is my wish
And let me seek blessings from You alone.

Lord! Lighten for me this heavy burden
And ease for me the path that leads to You.

Lord! Be compassionate towards me and
Count me among the party of righteous.

Conceal my faults O Hider of all things
For I always expect the best from You.

Relieve me of my anguish and sorrow
For the sake of Muhammad[sa] and Ahmad[as].

A committed servant of my Imam
Lord, aid me, secretly and openly.

A GIFT FOR AN-NADWAH

بِسۡمِ اللّٰہِ الرَّحۡمٰنِ الرَّحِیۡمِ

نَحۡمَدُہٗ وَنُصَلِّیۡ عَلٰی رَسُوۡلِہِ الۡکَرِیۡمِ [1]

God's help comes with my every breath,
Where are the enlightened so that they might see?

Today, 2nd October, 1902, I received an announcement published by Ḥāfiẓ Muḥammad Yūsuf, pensioner, which was addressed to me. According to him, he has long averred that certain persons who intended to mislead others by falsely claiming to be prophets or messengers sent by God, lived for 23 years or more [after making their claim]; (23 years being the duration of the Holy Prophet's mission). He further writes that a close friend of his, Abū Isḥāq Muḥammad Dīn, has published a book, *Qaṭ'ul-Watīn*, in which he has catalogued the names of such false claimants and the length of time of their 'mission' with reference to historical sources. It appears that Ḥāfiẓ Ṣāḥib does not admit the validity of the

[1] In the name of Allah the Gracious the Merciful. We praise Him and invoke His blessings upon His noble Messenger[sa].

[Publishers]

Quranic verses لَوْ تَقَوَّلَ[2] and وَاِنْ يَّكُ كَاذِبًا فَعَلَيْهِ كَذِبُهٗ[3] nor does he want to. Rather they are rejected in *Qaṭ'ul-Watīn* and, in his and Muḥammad Dīn's view, the following verses are also abrogated and of scant significance:

وَقَدْ خَابَ مَنِ افْتَرٰی[4]۔ اِنَّ الَّذِیْنَ یَفْتَرُوْنَ عَلَی اللّٰہِ الْکَذِبَ لَا یُفْلِحُوْنَ[5]۔ فَبَدَّلَ الَّذِیْنَ ظَلَمُوْا قَوْلًا غَیْرَ الَّذِیْ قِیْلَ لَھُمْ فَاَنْزَلْنَا عَلَی الَّذِیْنَ ظَلَمُوْا رِجْزًا مِّنَ السَّمَآءِ۔[6]

All these verses, including the verse in which God says that if the Prophet[sa] had attributed lies to Him, He would have seized him and cut his jugular vein, are seemingly dismissed in *Qaṭ'ul-Watīn*. Thus, according to Ḥāfiẓ Ṣāḥib, the warnings God issued in them are invalid and even if some Prophets had made false claims—God forbid—they would not have been destroyed. He

---

[2] [The verses say] And if he had falsely *attributed* even a trivial statement to Us, We would surely have seized him by the right hand,—*Al-Ḥāqqah*, 69:45-46 [Publishers]

[3] And if he be a liar, on him will be *the sin of* his lie;—*Al-Mu'min*, 40:29 [Publishers]

[4] And surely, he who forges a lie shall perish.—*Ṭā Hā*, 20:62 [Publishers]

[5] Surely, those who forge a lie against Allah do not prosper. —An-*Naḥl*, 16:117 [Publishers]

[6] The transgressors changed *it* for a word other than that which was said to them. So We sent down upon the transgressors a punishment from heaven,—*Al-Baqarah*, 2:60 [Publishers]

thus posits that there are no provisions in the governance of God against liars, creating a vacuum for all manner of deceit.[7] Accordingly, had any of the Prophets spoken falsehoods about God, they would not have been held accountable for it in this life. This also carries the implication that the laws of man are superior to those of God; for they are at least framed with provisions to apprehend and punish those who produce false testimony. Consequently, as far as Ḥāfiẓ Ṣāḥib is concerned, it is not a miracle that the Holy Prophet[sa] was granted a 23 year period for the completion of the revelation of the Holy Quran, that his life was safeguarded

---

7 In Ḥāfiẓ Ṣāḥib's view, God supports false claimants to the extent that despite the maximum efforts of their opponents, they remain alive long enough to fully establish their religion. If this premise were accepted, then there could not exist any fair or indispensible means for verifying the claims of the Prophets and the distinction between truth and falsehood would forever be blurred by a cloud of uncertainty. Thus it is immediately clear that blessing a Prophet with a long life and helping him sow the seed of his religion in the earth, despite the many ill-intentions and intrigues of his opponents, is a miracle which God performs for His true and perfect Messengers. But if we were to suppose that His favour also extended to false claimants, then these miracles would lose their legitimacy and a true Prophet would have no distinction. How incredible! Ḥāfiẓ Ṣāḥib has with one stroke sought to ruin the foundation of Islam. Is this what it means to be a Ḥāfiẓ? [Author]

from the attacks of his opponents and that he died in accordance with the Divine Will once his life had been completed. It has been prophesied that I too will be granted approximately 80 years in order to complete my mission. But as far as he is concerned, the fulfilment of such prophecies cannot be considered a sign of a claimant's truth. Under the dictates of his religion, no amount of Divine protection can establish the truthfulness of either the Holy Prophet[sa] or myself, because it is also possible for liars to fall within its purview. But, if this were accepted, the whole of the teaching of the Holy Quran, which declares that liars will be caught, disgraced, ruined and made to fail, would have to be considered false.

One's intellect can readily accept the idea, as found in the earlier scriptures that a person who strives to destroy the works of God should himself perish. But, in Ḥāfiẓ Ṣāḥib's opinion, there have been many people who have falsely claimed to be Prophets and the recipients of Divine revelation and have persisted in their claim for as long as thirty years. During this time, they continuously asserted their truth and fabricated revelations until their dying breath and departed this life in a state of disbelief. God prolonged their lives and allowed their work to flourish and did not punish them. Moreover, there is no evidence to suggest that they repented or publicly expressed their remorse so as to let the people know that they had returned to the fold of Islam.

Ḥāfiẓ Ṣāḥib states that sufficient proof of this can be found in *Qaṭ'ul-Watīn*. He also writes that he does not wish to receive the 500 rupee reward. Instead he desires that at the annual gathering of the *Nadwatul-Ulema* beginning on 9th October, 1902, in Amritsar, which will be attended by some of India's most renowned scholars, I should promise to repent if the historical authenticity of the examples cited in *Qaṭ'ul-Watīn* is accepted by the designated arbiters i.e. the *Nadwatul-Ulema*. That is, if they decide that my case is similar to that of other liars who claimed to have received Divine revelations, recorded them and spread news of them throughout the world and fabricated lies against God, and yet they were not destroyed. On the contrary, like me, they were blessed with a community of followers. If this be how they are persuaded I should repent before their gathering.

I would happily let the *Nadwatul-Ulema* arbitrate between Ḥāfiẓ Ṣāḥib and myself if God had blessed them with the necessary foresight, if they were just, righteous and had sufficient time to thoroughly investigate our respective claims. But, since I am given to doubt regarding their [earnestness and judicial faculty], I have decided not to make the journey to Amritsar. In truth, I do not esteem any of them as righteous, (if in the future God brings a change to their character, it will be out of His grace), nor do I believe them to possess knowledge of Quranic truths, for such understanding rests on the Quranic principle لَا يَمَسُّهٗۤ اِلَّا الۡمُطَهَّرُوۡنَ[8]. With this in mind, how can I accept their arbitration?

Instead, if some of their *ulema* were to come to Qadian, with the purpose of seeking the truth, I could communicate my message to them in person. Otherwise the work of God continues and cannot be halted by anyone. Surely there is no sense in seeking judgement from one's adversaries.

Nevertheless, I will take the opportunity, which Ḥāfiẓ Ṣāḥib's announcement has provided me, to convey my message to the people of *An-Nadwah*. Ḥāfiẓ Ṣāḥib should know that the less than cogent accounts found in *Qaṭ'ul-Watīn* about false claimants of Prophethood, cannot be considered plausible until it is established that these liars remained vigorous and adamant in their claim and were unrepentant. This can only be proved through historical sources which show that they died in a state of falsehood, their funeral prayer was not led by a Muslim [on account of their being outside the pale of

[8] None shall touch [it] except those who are purified.—*Al-Wāqi'ah*, 56:80 [Publishers]

Islam], and that they were not buried in a Muslim cemetery. Furthermore, a book or record of their lies, which they considered to be the word of God, must be shown to exist somewhere so that one can inquire into whether their claims were categorical and whether they enunciated that they were Prophets in a real sense or as a reflection thereof. That is, in order to reach a proper understanding of how they perceived of their revelations, in so much as, whether they claimed that their revelations were from God every much as the revelations of past Prophets. If so, the verse تَقَوَّلَ[9] would also be applicable to them. It seems Ḥāfiẓ Ṣāḥib is unaware of the fact that conviction and certainty are intrinsic to the injunction contained in this verse.

As I have stated numerous times before, the words I speak most certainly emanate from God, in the same way that the Holy Quran and the Torah emanated from Him. I am a Prophet of God in a *Ẓillī* and *Burūzī*[10] sense. All Muslims are obligated to obey me in matters of religion and to accept me as the Promised Messiah. Those

---

[9] *Al-Ḥāqqah*, 69:45-46. [see page 10] [Publishers]

[10] The words *Ẓillī* and *Burūzī* signify that the Promised Messiah was not a Prophet in his own right but achieved the mantle of Prophethood by completely immersing himself into the person of the Holy Prophet[sa]. In this way he was a reflection of the Prophet's spiritual light. [Publishers]

who have received my message but do not accept me as their arbiter or as the Promised Messiah nor believe in the Divine origins of my revelation will be accountable for this in the heavens even if they are Muslims. For they have rejected that which they should have accepted at its proper time.

Not only do I claim that if I had been a liar I would have been destroyed, but I also affirm that, like David[as], Moses[as], Jesus[as] and the Holy Prophet[sa] my claim is true and God has testified to it with over 10,000 signs. The Holy Quran too has testified in my favour as has the Holy Prophet[sa]. The Prophets of the past and the Holy Quran have determined the time of my advent, which is this very age. Both the Heavens and the earth have borne witness to my truth and no Prophet has passed who has not testified for me. Ten thousand is a very conservative estimate for the signs I have just mentioned. Indeed, I swear by God, Who possesses my soul that if I were to write these signs in a tome, its pages would end but these signs would not. God says in His Holy scripture:

إِنْ يَّكُ كَاذِبًا فَعَلَيْهِ كَذِبُهٗ ۚ وَإِنْ يَّكُ صَادِقًا يُّصِبْكُمْ
بَعْضُ الَّذِيْ يَعِدُكُمْ ۭ إِنَّ اللّٰهَ لَا يَهْدِيْ مَنْ هُوَ مُسْرِفٌ كَذَّابٌ ﴿۲۹﴾[11]

That is, 'If he is a liar, he will perish before your eyes on

[11] *Al-Mu'min*, 40:29 [Publishers]

account of his lie. But if he is truthful, some among you will be the victims of his prophecies and will pass from this temporary existence before his eyes.' Why not test me and investigate my claim by the criterion found in the Book of God? Is it not true that the *maulawīs* left no stone unturned in their attempts to have me destroyed? They have worn themselves out in preparing a verdict of apostasy against me and have used so many invectives against me in their announcements that the profanity of their language has surpassed even that of the Shiites. Not only did they bring me before the courts time and time again, I was even [falsely] accused of murder. Those who were drawn towards me were subjected to such persecution that apart from the instances of torture endured by the companions of the Holy Prophet[sa], there is no other example of the abuse and cruelty they have had to suffer. Some of my followers who belonged to foreign lands were martyred in their native countries. Who can deny that vigorous efforts have been made to crush me and prevent people from coming to me? Many of these very *maulawīs* have been guilty of any number of shameful acts. They provided false information about me to the government in order to incite it against me. But what was the result of all this? Only my continued success. When my opponents rose to denounce me as a liar and an infidel and prophesied that they would soon destroy me, I did not have a large following. At the time, I had with me just a few people who could be counted on the fingers of a hand. Indeed, when *Barāhīn-e-Aḥmadiyyah* was being published, I was all alone. Who can show that I had even one follower? It was then that God blessed me with over fifty revelations in which I was told that despite my solitary state, the day beckoned when a whole world of followers would join me and I would attain such glory that kings would seek blessings from my garments for I was blessed. Holy is God, He does what He wills. [I was told] that He would spread my community throughout the world, that He would bless them, increase them and honour them in the earth for as long as they remained true to His covenant. Just think that I was alone when these prophecies that I have translated above were first published in *Barāhīn-e-Aḥmadiyyah*. It was then that God taught me the prayer رَبِّ لَا تَذَرْنِيْ فَرْدًا وَّ أَنْتَ خَيْرُ الْوٰرِثِيْنَ [12]. That is, 'My Lord! Do not leave me alone and You are the Best of Inheritors.' This Divinely revealed supplication is also recorded in *Barāhīn-e-Aḥmadiyyah* which thus became a witness to my anonymity at the time. But today, despite the best efforts of my opponents, over a hundred thousand people from all over have joined my Jamā'at. Is it not then a

---

[12] *Al-Anbiyā'*, 21:90 [Publishers]

miracle that all manner of deceit was employed in order to oppose and defeat me and conspiracies were hatched by the *maulawīs* and their ilk, but they failed in their designs? If this is not a miracle then let the pompously adorned *maulawīs* of the *Nadwah* please tell us what constitutes a miracle.

If I cannot perform miracles, I am a liar. If the death of the Son of Mary cannot be substantiated by the Holy Quran, I am a liar. If the Hadith of the *Mi'rāj*[13] does not show the Son of Mary residing among the souls of the dead, I am a liar. If the Holy Quran has not made it abundantly clear in *Sura An-Nūr* that the successors of this umma will come from within the umma itself, I am a liar. If the Holy Quran has not referred to me as the Son of Mary, I am a liar.

Mortal souls! Is it not a miracle that, despite the best efforts of my opponents, the prophecies recorded in *Barāhīn-e-Aḥmadiyyah* some twenty-two years ago have been fulfilled? No one can prove that even one person was with me at the time. But today, if all my followers were to come together and settle in one place, I am sure that that town would be larger than Amritsar.

---

[13] The ascent or night journey taken by the Holy Prophet[sa] to heaven. [Publishers]

What is more, this prophecy would not have been fulfilled as magnificently as it has been if I had not been so fiercely opposed by the *maulawīs*. Not only have I been exonerated in the light of the verse وَاِنْ يَّكُ كَاذِبًا فَعَلَيْهِ[14] but my truth has also been established by the fulfilment of the prophecies published in *Barāhīn-e-Aḥmadiyyah,* twenty-two years ago, and by the manner in which thousands of blessed and capable persons have joined me since. Let us now turn to the second part of the afore-mentioned verse which says:

وَاِنْ يَّكُ صَادِقًا يُّصِبْكُمْ بَعْضُ الَّذِىْ يَعِدُكُمْ[15]

These words have been fulfilled in a brilliant manner. God spoke to me and said اِنِّىْ مُهِيْنٌ مَّنْ اَرَادَ اِهَانَتَكَ i.e., 'Whosoever insults you will not die before he sees his own humiliation.' One should ask these *maulawīs* whether, by the Will of God, they have not been humiliated on account of their hostility towards me. Who among those who have hurled insults at me can say that the Quranic prophecy[16] يُصِبْكُمْ بَعْضُ الَّذِىْ يَعِدُكُمْ has not been fulfilled in my favour? By using the word بعض [some] the Holy Quran

---

[14] And if he be a liar, on him will be *the sin.—Al-Mu'min,* 40:29 [Publishers]

[15] But if he is truthful, then some of that which he threatens you with will *surely* befall you.—*Al-Mu'min,* 40:29 [Publishers]

[16] Ibid

has demonstrated that the example of a few is enough to establish the truth of prophetic warnings. In this particular case there is no shortage of examples. Is it not disgrace enough for my opponents that Ghulām Dastagīr met his end soon after cursing me in his book *Fatḥi-Raḥmānī* (p.27) and asking God to curse the one out of the two of us who was a liar.[17]

Muḥammad Ḥasan Bhīń wrote لَعْنَةُ اللّٰہِ عَلَی الْکَاذِبِیْنَ[18] with reference to me in his book, but met his end before he ever had the chance to complete it. Pīr Mehr 'Alī Shāh invoked the same curse on me. Soon after, he was accused of plagiarism for he stole the work of Muḥammad Ḥasan after his death, and falsely passed it off as his own.[19] He lied and named the book *Saif-e-Chishtiā'ī*.

---

[17] Think, is it not a miracle that the same *maulawī* who had obtained edicts of apostasy against me from the injudicious *maulawīs* of Mecca, fell victim to the *Mubāhalah*. [Author]

[18] Let the curse of Allah befall the liars. [Publishers]

[19] By accepting the criticism made by Muḥammad Ḥasan, Mehr 'Alī, rather absurdly, accused me of copying proverbs and sayings from other works such as *Muqāmāt-e-Ḥarīrī*. I did indeed reproduce them in my book but in the form of extracts or citations that cover no more than two or three lines. In the opinion of this vacuous man this was evidence of plagiarism. But the prophecy *اِنِّیْ مُھِیْنٌ مَّنْ اَرَادَ اِھَانَتَکَ loomed over him and he instead was found guilty of stealing a whole book. He lied and put his faith in false criticism and did not grasp the

Moreover, Muḥammad Ḥasan's critique of my book *I'jāzul-Masīḥ* was also flawed. He had yet to revise the text when he died. But Mehr 'Alī, who has no grasp of Arabic, blindly accepted his arguments as literal truths. How calamitous for him that his grand larceny was discovered. Despite professing to be the successor of a saint he told a deliberate lie and passed off as his own a book which contained mistakes so flagrant they verged on being offensive. Is the punishment of hell more furious than this shame and embarrassment?[20]

To extract my repentance, it will not suffice for Ḥāfiẓ Ṣāḥib to produce a past tract authored by a false claimant who categorically enunciates that the revelations

---

fact that it was without any merit whatsoever. Thus, he was guilty of three great sins. Is this not a miracle? [Author]

* Whosoever insults you will not die before he sees his own humiliation. [Publishers]

[20] I am currently writing a comprehensive book *Nuzūlul-Masīḥ*, which will in part discuss the issue of Mehr Alī's plagiarism, his ignorant acceptance of false criticism and his erroneous assertion that the Son of Mary is still alive and other such matters which result from ignorance and a lack of understanding. Eleven sections of the book have already been published. Soon, the hollow edifice of his particular school of thought will collapse around him and the rising cloud of dust and ash will hurt his eyes and bring misery upon him. [Author]

recorded in it are as certain and categorical as the verses of the Holy Quran, just as I claim with regard to my revelations. Ḥāfiẓ Ṣāḥib will also have to show that the author of the work died before seeing the error of his ways, was not buried in a Muslim cemetery and was not punished by the Almighty. Here I must state that Ḥāfiẓ Ṣāḥib will not under any circumstances be able to furnish these proofs. How can a false claimant of Prophethood be likened to me? I have been supported by numerous miracles. Know that if Ḥāfiẓ Ṣāḥib were to endeavour to show that false claimants of the past published their revelations for a period of 23 years and swore in the name of God that their revelations were authentic and of Divine origin, in the same manner as I have done, he would most certainly be thwarted in his quest. Even if, until his dying breath, he spends his life in this search and commissions another Abū Isḥāq Muḥammad Dīn to write a thousand *Qaṭ'ul-Watīns,* he will still be frustrated. As I have repeatedly said in my previous books, if I am a liar then let the curse of God befall me. How pitiful that I am compared to such liars. I have irrefutable evidence of my truth in the form of thousands of miracles which have been manifested and witnessed by thousands. The Holy Quran too is my witness. Then, have I no right to demand some sort of proof from Ḥāfiẓ Ṣāḥib regarding these false claimants? In whose favour was the Hadith of *Dār-e-Quṭnī* regarding the eclipses fulfilled? For whom did the plague strike in accordance with [the prophecy found in] authentic Traditions? For whom did the comet appear? For whom was the sign of Lekhrām and many others manifested? If the *Nadwatul-Ulema* wish to live commensurately with the grandiose name they have chosen for themselves and long for the truth, whether Ḥāfiẓ Ṣāḥib himself desires it or not, they should at the very least ask him under oath to prove that the period of revelation of past false claimants of prophethood lasted for the same time as the complete revelation of the Holy Quran, i.e., 23 years. He should also be directed to show that those claimants swore that they were prophets and that their revelation was as indubitable as the verses of the Holy Quran. Moreover, he should provide evidence of whether or not such people were considered apostates by the *ulema* of the time. If not, then, why not? Were the *ulema* so iniquitous and corrupt that they showed such negligence in matters of religion? He should also be asked to produce evidence of where these false claimants were buried, i.e., whether they were buried in Muslim or non-Muslim cemeteries and whether they were executed under

Muslim rule[21] or lived a life of peace and tranquillity. After demanding these proofs from Ḥāfiẓ Ṣāḥib, a select few *ulema* of *An-Nadwah* should come to Qadian to conduct an inquiry and to demand from me proofs of my miracles and the evidence found in the verses of the Holy Quran and the Hadith in support of my truth. If the evidence I present does not accord with the traditions and practices of the Prophets of the past, I will agree to have all my books burned. But the fact is that only men of God can go to such lengths [in their quest for the truth]. Why would the *ulema* of *Nadwah* inconvenience themselves in this way? Why should they fear God when they hold no anxieties regarding the afterlife?

The *ulema* of *Nadwah*, each and every one of them, should bear in mind that they will not dwell in this world forever. Death beckons them all. God watches from the heavens as they amuse themselves in the frivolities they call Islam, but He knows that this is not

---

[21] With regard to false claimants in Islamic states, it would not be enough for Ḥāfiẓ Ṣāḥib to prove that they were not buried in Muslim cemeteries or that their funeral prayers were not observed by other Muslims, but [He would also have to demonstrate to the *Nadwatul-Ulema*] that, because these claimants were apostates, they were killed [for both Ḥāfiẓ Ṣāḥib and the *Nadwatul-Ulema* believe that the punishment for apostasy is death]. However, if he provides evidence of this, he will contradict his own claim. [Author]

Islam. They delight in superficialities and are completely ignorant of the sublime profoundness [of faith]. This is not a service to Islam, rather a disservice. If they had eyes, they would see that a great sin has been committed in the world, for the Messiah sent by God has been rejected. Every last person will be made aware of this after they have passed away. And yet Ḥāfiẓ Ṣāḥib would frighten me by suggesting that if I do not go to Amritsar the whole world will consider my claim false. Ḥāfiẓ Ṣāḥib! Are the affairs of this world governed by you or by God? You already call me a liar; what more will you impute? What do I care for you or your world? God has power over every soul. Unfortunate Ḥāfiẓ! What do you know of the support God extends to me? Even if those who are jealous of me struggle to within an inch of their lives, they cannot halt my progress. My success is from God and is a fulfilment of His promises. It is not within the control of any human being. God has filled the towns and cities of India and the Punjab with members of my community. In the space of a few short years, over 100,000 people have pledged their allegiance to me. Do you still not realise whom the Heavens support?

In my estimation, close to ten thousand people have joined me just by virtue of [the sign] of the plague, and I believe that in a few years hence the earth will be filled with my followers. Ḥāfiẓ Ṣāḥib! Was it not you who once told me that Maulawī 'Abdullāh Ṣāḥib Ghaznawī used to say that a [Spiritual] light had descended on Qadian but his children had failed to see? How unfortunate that you have saddened the resting soul of 'Abdullāh Ṣāḥib. Must you have gone against his wishes? And is Muḥammad Ya'qūb not your brother? Would it not have been prudent to confer with him? For almost ten years he has exclaimed that Maulawī 'Abdullāh Ṣāḥib Ghaznawī told him that a light had appeared in Qadian and that that light was Ghulam Ahmad. He has informed me that he stands by his testimony and I possess letters from him to this effect. You call yourself a Ḥāfiẓ and yet you place no trust in God Who is the true Ḥāfiẓ [Protector]. Out of fear of your people, you resort to lies and falsehood. At times I think about the visions and revelations 'Abdullāh Ṣāḥib received and how they have long since been buried with him. Even you, who are his eminent successor, attach no value to them. وَالسَّلَامُ عَلٰى مَنِ اتَّبَعَ الْهُدٰى[22]

Mirza Ghulam Ahmad of Qadian
4th October, 1902

[22] Peace be on those who follow the Guidance. [Publishers]

A Reason to Rejoice for All Muslims and Those who Seek the Truth

The beliefs in Jesus' supernatural life, his bodily ascension to the heavens and the idea that his spirit resided with the souls of departed Prophets who had already entered paradise, directly contradict with the Quranic teaching and are a fallacy and a stain on Islam. [The persistence of these doctrines] has meant that for far too long, Muslims monotheists have been in the figurative debt of the idolaters of the West. As a consequence of their acceptance of these doctrines, ignorant Muslims have allowed their debt to swell with interest. In India, hundreds of thousands have turned their backs on Islam and been seized by the clasping hand of Christianity. They have no apparent way of repaying this debt. The Christians [have long taunted the Muslims] by saying that their Lord, Jesus Christ, manifested his divine power by ascending to the heavens with his physical body, whereas the Holy Prophet[sa] of Islam could not even take flight to reach Medina and was forced to hide for three days in the cave of *Thaur* before reaching his destination with great difficulty. Thereafter, he was to live for only another ten years before death and the grave beckoned. Now his remains lie [forever] buried beneath the earth. Jesus Christ, however, is alive in the heavens and will live for eternity. It is he who will return to earth and re-establish justice in the world. All those who do not accept him as God will be seized and cast into the fire of hell.

The situation seemed hopeless and the Muslims had little or no response to these gibes. They were continually shamed and humiliated. But today, the [falseness] of Jesus Christ's divinity has been exposed, and the myth of his ascension shattered. Firstly, there has been the discovery of numerous ancient medical texts written by the Romans, Greeks, Zoroastrians and Christians and later translated by the Muslims which contain the formula for the 'the Ointment of Jesus'. It is reported that this ointment was prepared for his crucifixion wounds. Also, there is the discovery of the tomb of Jesus[as] in Kashmir. Furthermore, a number of Persian and Arabic texts have come to light, some over a 1000 years old, that provide evidence of Jesus' death and his burial in Kashmir. However the latest news I have received in this regard has brought with it a day of jubilation for all Muslims. I am alluding to the discovery in Jerusalem of an old Hebraic document which bears the signature of Jesus' disciple Peter (the content of which I have already reproduced in my book *Noah's Ark*). This document contains evidence that Jesus died on this very earth almost fifty years after he was put on the cross.

It has been purchased by a Christian company for 250,000 rupees and has been verified as having been written by Peter. It would be naïve to cling to the idea that Jesus is still alive in the face of such clear and overwhelming evidence. One cannot deny the facts. Muslims! I congratulate you, for this is a day of triumph. Abandon your false beliefs and fashion your faith in accordance with the Holy Quran.

Let me reiterate that this final testimony is that of Jesus' closest disciple. In this document, he identifies himself as Peter; a servant of the son of Mary. He tells his age as 90 and is writing 3 years after the death of Jesus. Historically, both Jesus and Peter are understood to have been of similar ages and that at the time of the crucifixion Jesus was approximately 33 years old and Peter somewhere between 30 and 40. Both these facts have been accepted by renowned Christian scholars (see *Smith's Dictionary*, Vol. 3, p. 2446,[23] موڈی ٹیورس *New Testament History*, and other historical works on the subject). A number of notable experts on Christianity have examined this letter and declared it authentic. This discovery has brought with it a great deal of joy. As I have already mentioned, the letter has been valued so highly that the heirs of the holy man from whose library it was found were paid a handsome amount for it.

[23] The title of this book cannot be clearly identified probably due to a misprint in the first Urdu edition. [Publishers]

To my mind further evidence of the authenticity of this letter lies in the fact that it emerged from the library of a Roman Catholic who believed not only in the divinity of Christ but also of Mary. He had kept it only as an ancient relic. Because it is written in Ancient Hebraic and uses archaic terms he was unaware of its actual import. This too is evidence [of the document's authenticity]. Besides the testimony found in Peter's letter, [we already know that] there were particular sects among the early Christians who believed that Jesus was taken off the cross in a state of unconsciousness which resembled death and brought to a sepulchre, where for three days he was nursed back to health. Afterwards he left for another land where he lived for many years. Details of these beliefs can be found in certain European books. Among them are *New Life of Jesus* by Strauss, *Modern Doubt and Christian Belief* and *Supernatural Religion*. I have quoted excerpts from these works in *Tuḥfah-e-Golarhwiyyah.*

Mirza Ghulam Ahmad of Qadian
6th October, 1902

INDEX

A

Abū Isḥāq Muḥammad Dīn 9, 25
Amritsar 13, 14, 21, 27

B

Barāhīn-e-Aḥmadiyyah (by the Promised Messiah[as]) 19, 20
Bhīń, Muḥammad Ḥasan 22
Burūzī 16

C

Christianity/Christians 33, 35

D

Dār-e-Quṭnī 25
David[as] 17

F

Fatḥi-Raḥmānī (by Ghulām Dastagīr) 22

G

Ghaznawī, Maulawī 'Abdullāh Ṣāḥib 28
Ghulām Dastagīr 22
Greeks 32

I

I'jāzul-Masīḥ (by the Promised Messiah[as]) 23

J

Jerusalem 33
Jesus[as] 2, 17, 31, 32, 33
Ointment of 32
was buried in Kashmir 32

K

Kashmir
Jesus' tomb in 32

L

Lekhrām 25

M

Mary[as] 34
Medina 31
Mehr 'Alī Shāh, Pīr 22
Mi'rāj, night of
the Holy Prophet[sa] saw Jesus[as] among the souls of the dead on 20
Modern Doubt and Christian Belief 35
Moses[as] 17
Muḥammad Yūsuf, Ḥāfiẓ 9
Muhammad[sa], the Holy Prophet 11, 12, 16, 17, 20, 31
Companions of 18
Muqāmāt-e-Ḥarīrī 23

N

Nāṣir Nawāb, Mīr 5

New Life of Jesus by Strauss 34
Noah's Ark (by the Promised Messiah[as]) 5, 33
Nuzūlul-Masīḥ (by the Promised Messiah[as]) 23

P

Peter, the Apostle 33

Q

Qadian .... ii, 14, 26, 28, 29, 35
Qaṭ'ul-Watīn (by Abū Isḥāq Muḥammad Dīn) 9, 10, 11, 13, 15
Quran, the Holy
  verses of
    Al-Anbiyā', 90 19
    Al-Baqarah, 60 10
    Al-Ḥāqqah, 45 .... 10, 15
    Al-Mu'min, 29 .... 10, 17, 21
    Al-Wāqi'ah, 80 14
    An-Naḥl, 117 10
    An-Nūr 20
    Ṭā Hā, 62 10

R

Roman Catholic 34
Romans 32

S

Saif-e-Chishtiā'ī [by Mehr 'Alī Shāh, Pīr] 22
Shiites 18
Smith's Dictionary 33
Supernatural Religion 35

T

Thaur, Cave of.. 31

Y

Ya'qūb, Muḥammad 28

Z

Ẓillī.. 16
Zoroastrians.. 32